What Real Christianity Looks Like

Looks Like

A Study of the Parables

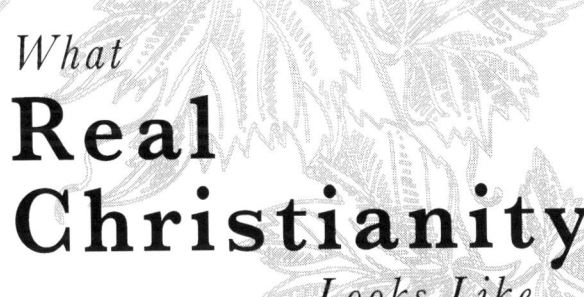

What
Real
Christianity
Looks Like

A Study of the Parables

Heritage Press
Florence, Alabama

What Real Christianity Looks Like
A Study of the Parables

Copyright © 2016 Heritage Christian University

Cover by: Robin N. Barrier

ISBN-13: 978-1533428813
ISBN-10: 1533428816

Published by Heritage Press
P.O. Box HCU, Florence AL 35630

A Message From
THE PRESIDENT

Welcome to the second edition of the Berean Study Series. This effort is intended to provide a valuable resource for congregations like yours. It is our desire to be of greater service to churches, year after year, by providing practical, useful and uplifting biblical materials at no cost to the church.

We were thrilled that over 400 churches took advantage of the inaugural Berean Study Series last year!

We hope you enjoy and benefit from this year's study. May God bless you in your daily walk as you apply the teachings of Christ with much thought and practice.

Sincerely,

Dennis Jones

BEREAN STUDY SERIES

The Berean Study Series

TABLE OF CONTENTS

Introduction

The Western world has grown tired of Christianity. For close to two millennia, the Christian faith has dominated the identity and history of Europe and, latterly, America, but the past several decades have seen a sharp reversal. Congregations are shrinking, church buildings are vacant, and polls continue to show that more people are giving up the Christian label in favor of...well, nothing in particular: when it comes to religion, they choose 'none'. Such a cultural transition—such a rejection of Christianity—should drive believers back to Scripture to discover again what Jesus expected of His followers.

Other areas of the world have witnessed remarkable growth in adherents to Christianity. Africa and Asia are perhaps already the center of gravity for the Christian religion, at least in terms of numerical strength and vibrancy if not in terms of financial resources. As Christianity enters new cultures east and south of its traditional strongholds, we should, again, reconsider the qualities Jesus wanted His followers to develop.

[Introduction]

In short, the issue of what real Christianity looks like presses on believers from multiple sides. If we are going to maintain this historic faith, what does that faith look like in a changing world, and what will it look like a decade from now, or a century? Is the religion that is spreading around the globe now the same as what Jesus preached? We should not be surprised if masses of people in the West reject the message of Christ, since He assured us of that precise response (Matt 7:13–14), but we still might wonder whether America and Europe have turned away from the biblical faith or, perhaps, rather from some heartless perversion of that faith.

As a people committed to the restoration of New Testament Christianity in whatever time and whatever place, we advocate careful reflection on the New Testament's witness to the religion promoted by Jesus, and here the direct teachings of our Savior in the gospels seem an appropriate point of emphasis. Of course, we could study real Christianity by looking at the letters of Paul, or the Revelation of John, or the Acts of the Apostles, but we have chosen to concentrate on the teachings of Jesus Himself so that we may listen to "the author and finisher of our faith" (Heb 12:2). We are further zeroing in on His parables—some, not all—because our Lord used this form of discourse to lay bare many essential truths that He had come to reveal. That is not to say that the parables are easy to understand. In fact, Jesus said the opposite: He spoke in parables in order to hide certain truths from the crowd and reveal these truths only to those who searched. When the disciples asked Him why He spoke in parables (Matt 13:10), Jesus responded,

11 To you it has been granted to know the mysteries of the kingdom of heaven, but to them it has not been granted. 12 For whoever has, to him more shall be given, and he will have an abundance; but whoever does not have, even what he has shall be taken away from him. 13 Therefore I speak to them in parables; because while seeing they do not see, and while hearing they do not hear, nor do they understand. 14 In their case the prophecy of Isaiah is being fulfilled, which says, "You will keep on hearing, but will not understand; You will keep on seeing, but will not perceive; 15 For the heart of this people has become dull, with their ears they scarcely hear, and they have closed their eyes, otherwise they would see with their eyes, hear with their ears, and understand with their heart and return, and I would heal them." 16 But blessed are your eyes, because they see; and your ears, because they hear. 17 For truly I say to you that many prophets and righteous men desired to see what you

*see, and did not see it, and to hear what
you hear, and did not hear it.*

Jesus explains that His parables fulfill the
commission of Isaiah to speak to people in such
a way that they would continue in their unbelief
(Isa 6:9–10). We might compare this hard saying
to the Lord's counsel that we should not toss our
pearls before swine (Matt 7:6). Jesus says that He
is using the parables to conceal His message from
all but those who see beyond the surface. Real
Christianity digs deep.

We do have an advantage over the first-century
crowds, however; we know more about Jesus than
they did. We know how His life will turn out, that
this Messiah will die on a cross, and we recognize
that that basic fact turns everything upside down so
that, in Christianity, necessarily the first will be last
and the last will be first. This insight should guide
every reading of the parables. But we also know
that the parables have a deeper significance, that
they are simple stories about profound truths, and
we know that because in this same passage from
Matthew Jesus says as much. And He goes on to
provide an example of interpretation, expounding
the Parable of the Sower in terms of the different
responses people have to the gospel. If we
persistently seek the meanings of the parables, we
have assurance that we will find.

However difficult the parables are to understand, they are much more difficult to put into practice. Lessons about mercy and compassion, or responsibility and preparation, or joy and hope, or inclusion and generosity, have resounded in church auditoriums every week from time immemorial, and yet these very character traits prove to be perpetually elusive for many. If the West has rejected Christianity, one may still wonder whether they have really rejected mercy, preparation, hope, inclusion, or whether these are not the values they associate with Christianity. If the answer to that last question is negative, the church has work to do.

An Ancient Near Eastern "Sacred" Tree from Assyria; like the Mustard Tree of Mark 4. Photo Credit: Jeremy Barrier

This "sacred tree" was found in a palace of King Ashurnasirpal of Assyria, 865–860 BC, in Nimrud. This sacred tree was one of many amongst eagle headed spirits and sacred trees in room F, panels 3–4 in the northwest palace. It is now housed in the British Museum (London).

Chapter 1

Endless Possibilities
The Parable of the Mustard Seed
{Mark 4:30-32}
Jeremy Barrier

One Main Thing

The possibilities are endless with God...

Introduction

What is it like?

Some things are simply too difficult to put in to words. I remember several years back, when my wife, Robin, and I were expecting our first child, and we were overflowing with anticipation and excitement about the prospects of parenthood. Amazingly enough, my brother, Joey, and his wife, Anna, shared the same due date with Robin for the anticipated birth of their daughter! I remember the day vividly, when Robin and I arrived at the hospital to visit Joey and Anna who "beat us to the punch" a few days before our son. I was anxious to know what I was about to experience, so I asked my brother "So, Joey, what is it like? How does it feel?" He was speechless for a moment before finally lifting his lowered eyes to look at me face to face. He then said quietly with moistened eyes, "I just don't know how God could do it. I don't know how He could have sent His Son..." The feeling for the occasion was simply too great to even put into words. Not just the feeling of being a parent, but the discovery he was making in the love of God simultaneously. Wow!

I'm amazed when I pick up Mark's gospel and we find Jesus saying to his disciples, "To what shall we compare the Kingdom of God...To what shall I liken it?" Here we find Jesus, the messenger and Son of God, and He is struggling to put into words how He would describe the Kingdom of God. How does one speak of the heavens, the reign of God, or the sovereignty of a benevolent and loving father? How does one express the deep emotion of something so magnificent that words can't express it?

Setting

The Underdog

As you probably know by this point, the parables are those beautiful little stories where God does attempt to communicate in words the feeling and ideas of God's reign, while also trying to situate us within it! How intimidating. In the case of Mark 4:30–32 (compare Matt 13:31; Luke 13:18–19), Jesus gives a universal illustration. Who doesn't know about seeds, dirt, trees, birds, and other small woodland creatures? This parable is a deceptively simple little story. In our Bibles today, the story itself lasts only three verses, but the punch, when adequately appreciated, has outlasted two millennia of interpretation by the "faithful." In this case, the simplicity of the story is apparent. In the language of hyperbole, Jesus gives a story about the underdog who overcomes. It is a message about how the "smallest" becomes the "greatest." This is an encouraging story for the ages. We all deeply love rooting for underdogs and seeing them conquer in the end. It is the football team greatly outmatched by their opponent, but somehow in the last moments of the game they pull off the 'hail mary' and win! We, as readers, are immediately able to discern this parable and we love it.

Interpretation

The Mustard Bush

However, at this stage, the echoing words of Jesus grab my attention as He so often said, almost scornfully, addressing His many multitudes of male and female followers, always addressing them in the more formal and socially appropriate masculine voice: "He who has ears to hear, let him hear." "Hear what?", you might ask. Indeed, the parable does have deeper dimensions to it. I have personally asked thousands of Christians on four different continents what they know about horticulture or plant husbandry, especially in regard to the planting and growing of mustard seeds. Only in Vietnam have I crossed paths with readers who actually grow mustard and were aware that mustard seeds grow into bushes and not trees! That's right, one might think Jesus has misled us on two counts in this story. First, the mustard seed is not the smallest of all of the seeds and secondly it does not grow into a tree! True, Mark mentions shrubs (not literally trees), but the story is elaborated further in Matthew and Luke giving us "trees" with great branches. It especially does not put forth branches for the birds! Now we are getting somewhere with Jesus' perplexing story.

Our own unfamiliarity with the flora of Palestine has caused us to miss an important detail. Jesus' hearers did know about mustard seeds and mustard bushes; thus, the parable would have taken on greater (shall we say even apocalyptic) proportions. What I am hinting at are the references to Scripture that Jesus embeds in His story. He quickly cites the examples of the great, old growth, trees of Scripture. The massive trees of the ancient near east, possibly even like those of the great "Cedars of Lebanon," that become home to the birds and shade to the weary traveler. These trees played a prominent role in an arid world that did not often see such visual demonstrations of strength, power, security, and dependability. In fact, we see the trees in Genesis 1-3 and realize that they bring even life and knowledge. Then we find the prophets of God recall them, comparing both kings and Israel alike to them (Ezek 17:23; 31:6; Ps 103:12 [LXX]; Dan 4:9, 18). These trees are not ordinary trees, but they represent the might and supremacy of God. A supremacy, that by the time of the persecutions of the first disciples of Jesus had become symbols of God's heavenly home, the New Jerusalem, as recalled in Rev 21–22. Jesus was challenging His hearers to imagine the impossible. Tiny mustard seeds growing, not into just bushes, but the old growth trees of Eden that provide shade for the birds and symbolize the might of kings!

Application

Trust Me, I Know What I Am Doing!

Here comes the "double take." The story is not merely a good story about the underdog. It is about people accomplishing the impossible. In Scripture, through faith, we overcome odds that cannot, should not, and never will be overcome... except...yes, that it is the amazing, punctiliar, impossible-made-possible God of Scripture! When God reigns in my life, God makes things happen that cannot happen otherwise. It doesn't mean that we can subvert God's will to ours, but He subverts our will to His! There have been so many marriages that would "never make it", but then the spouses submit to God and they "miraculously" make it! I am talking about all of the thousands of problems we face in life and there is simply no clear solution for them. We are trapped. We are fenced in. We are going to lose. Then enters the reign of God in our lives and the possibilities for deliverance change dramatically. Jesus is challenging us to trust Him! He is looking at us with deeply loving eyes and saying, "Please, trust me, I know what I'm doing!"

Conclusion

Recently, I had the chance to sit down with a few—only a few—of the Christians who live in Hanoi, Vietnam. The church in Vietnam was battered and almost crushed in 1975, following the Fall of Saigon on that sad day in April. "Crushed, but not destroyed...", if I may borrow Paul's memorable words (2 Cor 4:9). One of the Vietnamese Christians had brought her cousin with her who had never been able to sit and speak with those who believed in any god, let alone with Christians. As we sat for the next three hours discussing and explaining the God of the creation, I was amazed by the entire exchange. She was very anxious to learn about God! The young lady was aware and could see the 'signature' left on His handiwork that we call the Earth and could be seen all throughout the cosmos, made by a sovereign God. Indeed the ink was still not even dry from His signing! At the end of the day, we, even like the many of Hanoi, are aware that we are living in God's dominion. Sometimes the pains, the struggles, the realities of life weigh us down, and we forget that the one who set it all in motion is also seeking to weave our life into the grand drama called life. The challenge is for us. Will we trust Him? Will we be a part of God's reign? Will we allow God to do the impossible in our lives? Will we allow God to make us grow beyond our wildest expectations? The choice is ours.

Discussion

1. If you were asked to describe what it feels like to love to someone who says he or she has never loved, how would you describe it?

Is it difficult to fully explain love to others in words? Do you think it would have been difficult for Jesus to explain His kingdom to those around Him who had never seen it?

2. Have you ever grown any plants all the way up from seeds? What does it feel like? Is it difficult? Have you ever had any unexpected outcomes from your planting seeds?

3. If you were King for a day, what would you do? Would you feed everyone, give them good housing, or heal their illnesses? What do you think life would be like if God were "King for a day"?

Chapter 2

Joy

The Parable of the Old and New
{Luke 5:33-39}
Bill Bagents

One Main Thing

Life with Jesus brings a new joy and a fresh perspective.

Introduction

In addition to Luke 5:33–39, The Parable of the Old and New can also be read from Matthew 9:14–17 and Mark 2:16–22. While reading each account is wise, there is also wisdom in hearing Luke's account within its context.

The Parable of the Old and New came as Jesus responded to a series of questions—really criticisms and attacks—from the scribes and Pharisees, religious leaders of His day. The series of conflicts began in Luke 4:16–30 as Jesus read from Isaiah 61:1–2 declaring, "Today this Scripture is fulfilled in your hearing." Though the hearers "marveled at the gracious words" of Jesus, they took offense at the teaching that followed. That teaching was deemed too gracious toward Gentiles and too challenging toward the chosen nation. The anger of the crowd was so strong that they attempted to throw Jesus over a cliff. What a situation! Astonishment at a new presentation of God's grace was followed by murderous anger.

Conflict escalated in Luke 5:17–26 as Jesus healed a paralyzed man who was brought to Him by friends. The "problem" was not the healing; rather it was the manner of the healing. "When He saw their faith, He said to him, 'Man, your sins are forgiven you'" (Luke 5:20). While the healed man and the crowd glorified God and the witnesses were amazed and filled with fear, the scribes and Pharisees had a different reaction. Since only God can forgive sins and they did not see Jesus as the Son of God, they accused the Lord of blasphemy.

Additional conflict comes in Luke 5:27–32 as Jesus calls Levi, a tax collector, to follow Him. Not only that, Jesus ate and drank "with tax collectors and sinners." He treated outcasts as if they mattered. He announced, "I have not come to call the righteous, but sinners to repentance."

Given that context and the accusations that follow in Luke 6:2 and 7, we are hard pressed to view the question of Luke 5:33 as either innocent or information-seeking. "They"—the scribes and Pharisees—want Jesus to explain the conduct of His disciples. "Why do the disciples of John fast often and make prayers, and likewise those of the Pharisees, but Yours eat and drink?"

As He often did, Jesus began His response to their question with a question of His own. "Can you make the friends of the bridegroom fast when the bridegroom is with them?" (Luke 5:34). He presents His earthly ministry as a time of joy and celebration for His disciples.

Setting

It is commonly believed that putting fresh grape juice into old wineskins would lead to breakage as any degree of fermentation or expansion would not be tolerated by the somewhat dried and inflexible containers.

Concerning the question about fasting, numerous biblical texts support the implication of Luke 5:33 that fasting was commonly practiced during the first century. Jesus fasted before His temptation (Luke 4:1–2). He instructed His disciples to avoid abuses of fasting (Matt 6:16–18). The New Testament includes examples of fasting by Jews (Luke 2:37), Gentiles (Acts 10:30), and Christians (Acts 14:23). Fasting is often linked to prayer (Ps 35:1; Matt 12:21; Acts 13:3; 1 Cor 7:5).

Interpretation

The Gospel of Luke begins with a series of joy stories. There is joy for Zacharias and Elizabeth as the angel announces that they will have a son in their old age. There is joy for Mary, "highly favored" by God and "blessed among women," as she will give birth to the Messiah (1:22). Elizabeth's baby jumped for joy when Mary greeted her relative (1:44), and Luke documents the joy of the neighbors (1:58). The angel delivered "good tidings of great joy" to shepherds in the field (2:10). Aged Simeon and Anna found great joy in seeing the Messiah (2:25–29).

Joy in the presence of the Savior is one major reason that the disciples of Jesus did not fast like the disciples of John and of the Pharisees. Though Jesus was "a man of sorrows and acquainted with grief" (Isa 53:3) and He predicted His rejection before it came (Luke 4:23–24), He supported the joy that the disciples found in His person and His mission. He did not ask His disciples to conform to the behavioral traditions of the religious world around them.

The key reason for joy emphasized by this parable is the new age—the new life—being ushered in through the earthly ministry of Jesus Christ. To speak metaphorically, "There's a new sheriff in town, and He is like nothing ever seen before." More accurately, there was a new King in the world. His disciples realize something of this great truth, and that realization has changed their lives. The arrival of the Christ stirs their hearts to joy and celebration. There will be times of sorrow and mourning, but that time is not now.

The arrival and ministry of the Savior did not call for the tweaking or even the reformation of the status quo. It called for joy in the presence of the Savior and in the new life He offered.

What was and continues to be stunningly new about Jesus coming into this world?

- Joy (Luke 2:10–11). Joy within His very name: "And they shall call His name Immanuel, which is translated, "God with us" (Isa 7:14; Matt 1:23).
- Hope (1 John 3:1–4; Heb 6:13–20)
- Salvation (Luke 2:11; John 1:29; Acts 4:12)

- Peace (Luke 2:14; John 14:27)
- Reconciliation (Rom 5:1–11)
- Incredible promises (2 Pet 1:2–4; John 14:1–6)
- Unity (John 17:20-26; 1 Cor 12)
- Assurance (Rom 8)

Even before His public ministry, we read the following foreshadowing statements from Luke:

- "...Behold I bring you good tidings of great joy which will be to all people"(2:10).
- "For my eyes have seen Your salvation which You have prepared before the face of all peoples, a light to bring revelation to the Gentiles, and the glory of Your people Israel" (2:30–32).

Citing the widow of Zarephath and Naaman the Syrian as examples, Jesus reminded His fellow Jews that God loves people in every nation (Luke 4:23–27). The earthly ministry of Jesus focused on the Jews, but we get frequent reminders that God's plan was to open the door of salvation to all—Jew and Gentile alike. Matthew 28:18–20, Mark 16:15–16, and Acts 1:8 speak to this truth that would necessitate a new covenant between God and man. In God's time and way, the Israel of God would come to include "in every nation whoever fears Him and works righteousness..." (Acts 10:34–35; 11:18; 13:46–49).

Application

On a personal level, the Parable of the Old and New invites us to reflect on Jesus' ability to make us new—to give us new hearts and new minds. That stage is set by Luke 5:32: "I have not come to call the righteous, but sinners, to repentance." Because all sin (Rom 3:23), all are in need of rebirth (John 3:1–13). Jesus offers new birth and new life (John 1:11–13; 14:6; Eph 2:1–10). We love the mercies of God as expressed through Jesus. We find them "new every morning" as we hope in Him (Lam 3:22–24).

See Romans 6:4 for a beautiful description of this new heart and mind: "Therefore we were buried with Him through baptism into death, that just as Christ was raised from the dead by the glory of the Father, even so we also should walk in newness of life." Colossians 2:12 and Galatians 2:20–21 document God's power to give new life.

We offer no apology for the peace, love, and joy that fills our hearts. Our joy is "in the Lord" (Phil

4:4). Our peace is "the peace of God" (4:7). Our worldview, mindset, and attitude flow from our trust in God (4:9).

We appreciate the balance and wisdom of Scripture. This parable emphasizes joy, but hints at the inevitable ebb and flow of life (Luke 5:34–35). It emphasizes the new life ushered in by Jesus, but it acknowledges value in "the old" as well (5:39).

Conclusion

Life with Jesus brings a new joy and a fresh perspective. We serve the Master from happy hearts. We do not judge ourselves or allow ourselves to be judged by human standards and expectations. We know the joy of serving and loving only one Lord.

Discussion

1. How does the context of this parable contribute toward our understanding of it?

2. Of all the amazing new blessings and opportunities that Jesus brought to this world, which amazes and impresses you most? Why?

3. Why was it so difficult for the people

of Jesus' day to understand the newness
of His gospel?

4. How do we keep the gospel ever new in
our hearts? Why is it important that we do?

Chapter 3

Compassion

The Parable of the Good Samaritan
{Luke 10:25-37}
Jim Collins

One Main Thing

Real Christian living is about demonstrating love and compassion.

Introduction

The Parable of the Good Samaritan who gave aid to a stranger is one that has left an indelible imprint on the conscience of mankind. Luke is the only writer to record this particular message of Jesus. This beautiful story illustrates the type of love and compassion God wants each Christian to have. He desires that we demonstrate love and compassion for each other, our neighbors, strangers, and even enemies (Matt 5:43–44).

Setting

Jesus was asked the question by a certain lawyer who stood up and was testing Him saying, "Teacher, what shall we do to inherit eternal life?" Jesus responded, "What is written in the law? What is your reading of it?" So He answered and said, "You shall love the Lord your God with all your heart, with all your soul, with all your strength, and with all your mind, and your neighbor as yourself" (Luke 10:25–27, NKJV).

We know this was the lawyer's attempt to trap Jesus, to get Him to say something that could be used against Him. Why? The lawyer was one of those who was supposed to know and practice the law. The lawyer quotes Deuteronomy 6:5 and Leviticus 19:18. He knew what the law required and was able to quote it correctly. Jesus commends his ability to quote the Scripture and states, "You have answered rightly: do this and you will live." However, now the lawyer wishes to justify his motives by asking another question. "Who is my neighbor?" Jesus explains with the Parable of the Good Samaritan.

The conflict and tension in this parable should cause each one of us to think about what God really wants from us. Jesus' reply to the lawyer was a tough statement. It can be equated with the statement of Jesus in Matthew 5:43–44 where He says, "You have heard that it was said, 'You shall love your neighbor and hate your enemy.' But I say to you, love your enemies, bless those who curse you, and pray for those who spitefully use you and persecute you."

When I read these words, I think they are surely "hard sayings of Jesus." This thought prompts me to ask the question, "Lord, what do you mean, 'love my enemies'? Are you sure? This is too hard, too difficult, it is beyond my ability. Lord, surely you are not expecting me to grow to this level!" Jesus was laying the foundation of Christian principles. In context, He was describing how the scribes and Pharisees had twisted the original meaning and intent of the Scriptures. Now He is correcting their teaching.

The lawyer's motive wasn't right from the start. I wonder how often we Christians have failed to have the right attitude and motive in doing God's will.

Interpretation

The parable lists four different travelers who venture down the road between Jerusalem and Jericho. The road was famous for its many dangerous spots. Jerusalem sits in the hills, about 2,300 feet above sea level. Jericho lies on a low plain near the Dead Sea, about 1,100 feet below sea level. The road between the two cities covers only seventeen miles but descends about 3,400 feet. It was a winding path and dropped sharply, causing a zigzag trail that was extremely hazardous for travelers. The first-century Jewish historian Josephus describes the road as "desolate and rocky." In the early fifth century, the biblical scholar Jerome mentioned that bandits still lurked on that path.[1]

We will consider each of the four travelers next.

Application

The four travelers in this parable illustrate different attitudes and experiences that provide valuable points of reflection for the modern Christian. The first of the travelers is the victim. He was most likely a Jew who fell among thieves who took his clothes, injured him, leaving him half dead and at the mercy of animals and elements.

---

[1] Jerome, *Commentary on Jeremiah*, trans. Michael Graves, Ancient Christian Texts (Downers Grove, IL: IVP, 2011), 20.

The second traveler was a priest, one who knew the law, was to teach the law and of course put it into practice. He looked at the injured man, and passed by on the other side of the road. So what could possibly be his excuse? Perhaps he was going up to Jerusalem to serve in the temple. According to scripture, "he who touches a dead body of anyone shall be unclean seven days" (Num 19:11). Therefore, if he touched the body and the man was dead he would have to return home unable to complete his worship. How would we equate that in the twenty-first century? As we are all priests of God (1 Pet 2:9) and study the scriptures, we might think about times when we're on our way to worship services. We're dressed up in our Sunday attire, we notice someone pulled over to the side of the road with the hood of the car raised, and we kind of look the other way. Why? We don't want to be late to worship services. There is the possibility of getting our Sunday clothes dirty and we won't have time to go home and change. We move over to pass as the law requires and go on by.

The third traveler was a Levite, a deeply religious man who wore around his wrist a little leather box, in which were pieces of paper with scripture written on them (think Deut 6:4–9). He knew the law, but chose to justify himself by saying, "who is my neighbor." How does this scripture function today? We may be like the Levite and know what the word says, but we don't really want to put it into practice. Therefore, we make excuses, employ rationalization, or invoke justification for not being active in participation. We might even want to blame the victim for putting himself in danger by traveling alone on a dangerous road. We might justify our reasoning for not helping the poor, the helpless, the orphan, the widow, by rationalizing they are in desperate conditions because of their own choices and failure to make good decisions.

Finally, the fourth traveler was the Samaritan. He immediately went to the injured man with compassion, bandaged his wounds, poured on oil and wine. He then placed him on his own animal, took him to an inn, and took care of him personally. The next day, he gave the innkeeper money for the Samaritan's keeping, and said "Take care of him; and whatever more you spend, when I come again, I will repay you." In regard to the Samaritan, he obviously was very caring and compassionate. He did what the Jewish Priest and Levite should have done. The sting of this parable lies in the fact that not only did the orthodox religious leaders not fulfill one of the most important commandments of the Torah—as the question and answer preceding this parable indicate (Luke 10:25–27)—but the one who did was a Samaritan, whom Jews usually regarded (with some justification! cf. John 4:22) as members of a corrupted religion.

Conclusion

Christianity is about loving your neighbor, being compassionate to the less fortunate, and having a heart to help the helpless and downtrodden. Christianity is not just a name to use or badge of honor to wear, it is more! Jesus said to the lawyer, "So which of these three do you think was a neighbor to him who fell among the thieves?" And he said, "He who showed mercy to him." Then Jesus said to him, "Go and do likewise."

Which one of these travelers describes you? Remember Jesus asked the question in relationship to loving the Lord with all your being and your neighbor as yourself. When we can love each other, have compassion on those who need compassion, we will be treating others as we would treat ourselves and becoming more like Jesus (Phil 2:1–8). In that way, we can be Christians in more than name.

Discussion

1. Does the challenge Jesus issued to the lawyer mean that we should help those

who squander their financial resources on drinking, gambling, drugs, or some other vice?

2. Does the teaching of Jesus exempt us from helping any certain nationality, such as the Arab, African, or Middle-Eastern refugee?

3. Can our sorrow for these people exist only as an emotion? Is it okay to feel compassion without actually helping?

4. Will self-justification for failure to help be acceptable on judgment day?

5. How does this parable apply today in the context of debates over immigration, whether legal or illegal? Would Jesus want us to help the illegal immigrant?

6. Is there middle ground with some of the solutions to these questions?

Chapter 4

Using Your Talents
The Parable of the Talents
{Matthew 25:14-30}
Ed Gallagher

One Main Thing

Failing to use the resources God has given us results from fear and laziness and leads to condemnation.

Introduction

"Every good thing given and every perfect gift is from above, coming down from the Father of lights, with whom there is no variation or shifting shadow" (James 1:17).

Christians are a blessed people, and these blessings come from God. We acknowledge that God "has blessed us with every spiritual blessing in the heavenly places in Christ" (Eph 1:3). Those blessings surely include redemption from sin and hope for a glorious future. The apostles also talked about other sorts of spiritual gifts that their readers needed to use for the benefit of others (cf. 1 Pet 4:10; Rom 12:3, 6; etc.). Paul explains extensively that the distribution of various spiritual gifts among the Corinthian believers was not designed to exalt individual Christians but to build up the body through love (1 Cor 12–14). Similarly, the apostle explains in Ephesians 4:11–16 that different believers have different functions and abilities so that the whole church may benefit.

Besides all these tremendous spiritual blessings, God also provides for our physical needs (cf. Matt 6:25–34). Indeed, American Christians in the twenty-first century can rightly claim that God has blessed us materially more than most people in world history could "ask or imagine" (cf. Eph 2:20). Perhaps followers of Christ have not reflected enough on what God intends for us to do with all this abundance of wealth. We may assume that He wants us to live comfortable lives, that the fact that we happened to be born in America as opposed to some other country with more primitive conditions was simply a lucky break on our part, or perhaps part of God's design to make life easy on us. Maybe we think of our wealth like the Corinthians thought about their spiritual powers: it's all for me.

The Parable of the Talents suggests a different interpretation.

Setting

Before His betrayal and crucifixion, Jesus spends time preparing His disciples for their life and ministry without His physical presence among them (Matt 24–25). He talks some about the destruction of Jerusalem that would occur in a few decades, and He talks about His own glorious return in judgment, His second coming. He repeatedly emphasizes that His disciples need to be ready for the coming judgment, because it will happen unexpectedly, like a thief in the night (24:42–44). They need to be faithful and responsible slaves who do their work diligently (24:45–51). They need to be like wise virgins who, with adequate oil for their lamps, are ready to meet the bridegroom (25:1–13). They need to be like the slaves who use their master's resources for his advantage rather than hide it in the ground (25:14–30).

The Parable of the Talents—in its literal meaning— has to do with money. A talent was a unit of weight, about 50–75 lbs. The value of a talent varied depending on what material it was—gold, silver, copper—but it was always an enormous sum of money. A talent of gold, for instance, would have been equivalent to about 6,000 denarii, which was the standard day's wage for a laborer (cf. Matt 20:1–16).[1] In 2016, 50 lbs. of gold would cost around a million dollars, so we can imagine the slave receiving five talents to have about five million dollars at his disposal. A similar parable is found in Luke 19:11–27, the Parable of the Pounds, but this parable seems to have a different point, and the unit of currency is much smaller: a mina or "pound" is about 100 denarii.

Interpretation

This parable is about using the gifts that God has provided. We often (correctly) think about this parable as an admonition to use our abilities, and this interpretation is helped along by the fact that the English word "talent" happens to mean "ability." In fact, the English word "talent" with this meaning originated in interpretations of this parable. Literally, the Greek word "talent" referred to money, but the parable uses this word to symbolize whatever gifts the Christian might possess.

Jesus says that each of the slaves receives talents in accordance with their abilities (25:15), an idea that corresponds to other biblical teaching regarding

---

[1] W. D. Davies and D. C. Allison, *A Critical and Exegetical Commentary on the Gospel According to Saint Matthew, 3 vols.*, International Critical Commentary (London: T&T Clark, 1988–97), 3.405.

spiritual gifts (1 Pet 4:10; Rom 12:6). This notion is a unique aspect of this parable that does not appear in the surrounding parables and teachings.

The first two slaves used their talents and profited by them. Jesus does not directly make an application from this point, but we might imagine that He intended for His followers to understand that they should use their abilities and resources for the benefit of others. He teaches this lesson directly on many occasions.[2] These slaves are rewarded by a lofty commendation and admittance to their master's joy (25:21, 23).

The third slave hid his talent in the ground because he was afraid of the master (vv. 24–25). The master also accuses the slave of being lazy (25:26), though the slave may have described himself as cautious. His fear of making a mistake with his talent paralyzed him, but his inactivity—his laziness—infuriated the master and led to the worst kind of punishment (v. 30). It seems that the master would have been less angry if the slave had used the talent in some way, even if his business venture resulted in a less successful return than the other slaves, or possibly even a loss. "A previous

---

[2] On money specifically, see Matt 6:3–4; 19:21; on wider use of resources, see 25:31–46.

parable implies that fearful inaction is unwarranted because God will forgive unwise action with his resources (18:23–25)."[3]

Application

This parable has significant application for the church today in two directions: faithfulness and diligence lead to great reward; fear and sloth lead to menacing punishment. These lessons are taught in any number of passages of Scripture. The distinctive element in this parable is the emphasis on the gifts given by God to each disciple in accordance with his or her ability, and the need for the disciple to put these gifts to use.

The Parable of the Talents implies that followers of Jesus—individually and collectively—need to identify the gifts given by their master and employ them. Many of us can identify wealth as one of the gifts given to us by God, and our master expects us to use this gift on behalf of others. Other gifts that we have might include various talents or opportunities; squandering them angers our master. Our children are gifts, and we must diligently and carefully mold them without wasting our opportunities. The church

---

[3] David L. Turner, *Matthew*, Baker Exegetical Commentary on the New Testament (Grand Rapids: Baker, 2008).

is a gift, and we must wisely and fearlessly deploy our human resources to the glory of God.

The wicked slave in the parable misuses his talent because of fear and laziness. You don't have to think too hard about the church today to recognize some of the same problems. There are often situations in which church leaders fail to act in a positive and bold way out of fear. This parable encourages us to question the wisdom of such inactivity and whether laziness might also be a factor. Sometimes, because of fear, we seek merely to hold on to what we have (the status quo) rather than work toward advancement. The master in this parable sees such fear as a mark of wickedness.

The fourth-century preacher John Chrysostom commented, "Do you see how sins of omission are also met with extreme rejection? It is not only the covetous, the active doer of evil things and the adulterer, but also the one who fails to do good."[4] The words of James 4:17 echo in our minds.

Gregory the Great from the sixth century reflected on the notion of hiding a talent in the earth and suggested that it represents "employing one's abilities in earthly affairs, failing to seek spiritual

---

[4] Manlio Simonetti, ed. *Matthew 14–28*, Ancient Christian Commentary on Scripture, New Testament (Downers Grove, IL: IVP, 2002), 229.

profit, never raising one's heart from earthly thoughts."[5] We may be able to recognize these sorts of qualities in those churchgoers who remain on the sidelines of commitment and whose behavior appears unaffected by the gospel. They squander their talent.

Even the slave with the single talent was expected to put that talent to good use. Just because a disciple might not have the same abilities or resources as someone else does not permit him or her to waste the gifts God has provided. The second slave did not gain as much as the first, but he was not for that reason given any less reward. He used what he had, and received praise equal to that of the one who had used his greater resources to gain greater profit.

Conclusion

If we can identify resources that God has given us, we had better also be prepared to identify ways that we are using them for His kingdom. When our master returns, He will ask what we've been up to. We need a better answer than maintaining the status quo.

---

[5] Simonetti, *Matthew*, 223.

Discussion

1. What resources has God put at your disposal? What about at your congregation's disposal?

2. In what ways has your congregation been good at deploying the resources God has given you? In what ways could you improve?

3. Why does fear often hinder good work in the church? What are we afraid of? How do we overcome this fear?

4. Describe how the master's reward to the two diligent slaves motivates you to live fearlessly.

Chapter 5

Mercy

The Parable of the Unmerciful Servant
{Matthew 18:21-31}
Arvy Dupuy

One Main Thing

What does real mercy look like?

Introduction

The parable that closes Matthew 18 is triggered by the question asked as the chapter begins. The disciples came to Jesus and asked "...who is the greatest in the kingdom?" In the typical human way of seeing community, determining our rank is often the first order of business. That's just the way we do things and see things. But in the community of Jesus, things operate differently. His is a world where the least is the greatest, the weak are strong, the first are last and the humble are rewarded. This upside down way of thinking, living, and acting are at the center of the chapter and drive the telling of this parable. In the text considered here, Jesus gives us His longest treatment of this often asked and still relevant topic, and His teaching should lead us to understand and view this issue in a way that is counter to human nature.

Setting

The organization of the story lends itself to the structure of a typical Jewish parable: arrangement by threes. There are three main participants: a king, a servant, and a fellow servant. There are also three scenes with three subsections or speakers in each:

> King's Accounting
> > Master-Servant-Master
> Servant's Accounting
> > Servant-Fellow Servant-Servant
> King's Response
> > Master-Servant-Servant

This structure attracts a reader's attention and engages imagination but would have also given an initial false sense of a Jewish setting. The Jewish audience on the day of this teaching would have been expecting the flow of the narrative to have the first two participants doing things wrong and the third individual, a good Jew, to make all things right by their actions. However, Jesus, ever the master teacher, throws them a curve ball from the onset.

The large sum of money presents problems for the setting; is this purely an imaginary event? That is entirely possible. Many would say the large sum of money is amplified to make a point and in no way corresponds to reality. The talent (the largest monetary denomination) and the denarius (the smallest) lent themselves to a natural contrast of extremes. Ten thousand, in the first century Jewish world, was the highest figure in which arithmetic was calculated.[1]

However, there are other clues in the text that would have allowed those listening that day to see an alternate understanding. The large sum of money could denote a royal situation. Certainly the amount involved would merit someone other than a common slave, maybe a high official or representative of the king. But under what circumstances would such an amount be due?

A king would normally contract out tax collections on farm lands under their control at an auction to the highest bidder. The arrangement could be very lucrative because the contractor, after adding on his percentage, could then subcontract the

---

[1] Donald Senior, "Matthew 18:21–35," *Interpretation* 41 (1987): 403–7, at 405.

actual collection to others. However, along with the potential windfall also came risk. What if the there is a drought? What if pestilence destroys the crops? In that outcome collections would be short; possibly woefully short.

Records indicate that Herod's total collection was only 900 talents.[2] However, Josephus tells of Joseph son of Tobias, a tax-farmer, who offers to collect taxes totaling 16,000 talents for the Egyptian King Ptolemy (Antiquities 12.175–76).[3] This leads to the probable conclusion that if the scenario was a tax farming situation the King would be Gentile not Jewish.[4] The servant begs for patience and says he will repay the entire huge amount. If he is understood as a collector of tax farming, the debt could be rolled to the next year's harvest, and the scenario seems plausible. The threat to throw him into prison was a normal punishment for failure to live up to a contract.

---

[2] Bernard Brandon Scott, "The King's Accounting: Matthew 18:23–34," *Journal of Biblical Literature* 104 (1985): 429–42, 432.

[3] J. Duncan M. Derrett, *Law in the New Testament* (London: Darton, Longman and Todd, 1970), 36n3.

[4] Martinus C. de Boer, "Ten Thousand Talents: Matthew's Interpretation and Redaction of the Parable of the Unforgiving Servant (Matt 18:23–35)," *Catholic Biblical Quarterly* 50 (1988): 214–32, at 217.

In addition, there are other elements of the teaching that indicate non-Jewish origin. The KJV renders v. 26, "he fell on his knees and worshipped him." No Jew would ever worship another person. However, Hellenistic kings were often thought to be divine. Furthermore, Jewish law forbade the sale of wife and children to settle a husband's debt, though that form of punishment was not unusual for Gentiles.[5] Lastly, choking someone was socially unacceptable among Jews (cf. 18:28).

All of this presents the possibility that the setting could have been based in actual events with Gentile participants. This conclusion is made even more believable as Jesus uses the preconceived prejudices by the Jews against Gentiles to draw the audience into the story and keep them engaged to see what happens next. The text deliberately creates this tension which keeps the reader from knowing which way things will go.

Interpretation

Typical of Matthew's style, this parable is a thinly veiled allegory. Also in line with several of Matthew's parables the end result is judgment.

---

[5] Joachim Jeremias, *The Parables of Jesus*, 2d ed. (New York: Scribner's, 1972), 211.

Reconciliation is another major theme. This parable is one of several instances in Matthew's gospel where an urgent appeal for reconciliation is found.

In the end this parable is about community: a word portrait of ideal community and what mercy really looks like, a place where concern for the alienated and marginalized dominate the narrative and reconciliation has no limits. The God revealed by Jesus here is a God of unimaginable compassion.

Forgiveness is a central consideration in this story, as well. Forgiveness here is not a matter of dealing with a personal insult or even verbal offense, as Peter surmises (18:21), but the matter at hand is financial: there is a debt that is owed. Clearly that debt is ours of our own making to God because of our sin.

The clear point of the parable is the contrast between the behavior of the King and the servant in all these areas.

Application

The appeal of Christ is for us as readers today to be challenged about our own behavior.

Forgiveness is urgent because we are a forgiven people. What the servant first experienced from the King, unconditional compassion, is the reality out of which he was expected to act, and the same is true for us. To love an enemy or show mercy in places and situations where it is least expected we will demonstrate the ultimate form of forgiveness and that in turn makes us a child of the God whose love is unexpected and unlimited.

Throughout the gospels, especially Matthew, we see mercy with warnings of judgment. The need for responsible action as the sign of authentic faith is a reoccurring theme and it is connected to our accounting before God in the end. The Christian life is not a matter of just good intentions, ritualistic performances, or wishful thinking; faith must be translated into just and compassionate acts. The experience of God's grace brings with it a responsibility to act graciously. Justice is not an option but an urgent demand flowing from the reality of the gospel.

The beauty of Jesus' teaching is that He sets up the Jewish audience (but also us today). They are thinking how cruel the Gentiles are in their affairs. But then there is the master's pity; how unexpected. All this is woven together to bring the audience into the narrative and have them invest emotionally in the outcome just as we must invest in others and be emotionally engaged about their eternal outcome.

Conclusion

This parable presents profound and living theology. A fundamental message of this parable is that the Christian must act on a basis of God's incalculable mercy to us. We must give out what we have been given. Real mercy is demonstrated, lived out, and shown. If someone were asked what real mercy looked like, would they think of you?

Discussion

1. How do you define mercy?

2. What words would you use to describe the opposite of mercy?

3. Why do you think the servant asked the King for more time and did not ask for the debt to be canceled?

4. What stereotypes do we struggle with today? Are religious and moral superiority two of those?

5. The servant was within his legal rights to ask for the debt from the fellow servant. Discuss rights and demands for justice in human terms versus God's terms.

— *58* —

6. How is the act of mercy, and not the amount of the debt, the element that is unexpected?

7. Discuss the master's act of mercy not representing simply a temporary and unrepeatable "exception" to the rule but the new rule.

8. What would be the results if your congregation lived by Jesus' teachings on mercy?

9. Why do you think emotions are so closely connected to mercy?

10. Describe a time someone has shown mercy to you.

Chapter 6

Taking Responsibility

The Parable of the Lost Son
{Matthew 15:11-24}
Philip Goad

One Main Thing

God is always ready to be in a relationship with the person who will take responsibility.

Introduction

We usually refer to it as the Parable of the Lost (or Prodigal) Son, even though it may be more about the son who never left home in the first place. Luke 15 features two parables about the way people should react when that which was lost has been found, and a third story about the way in which the Pharisees of Jesus' day reacted when sinners were being converted. In any event, there are also valuable lessons to be learned from the younger son who purposefully left. The story of his demise and return helps us better understand what it looks like to take responsibility.

[Taking Responsibility]

Setting

Jesus sets up a scenario in the parable that while unusual, was not completely unheard of in that day. The younger son in this wealthy family wants to leave home and asks for his inheritance immediately. While the father was under no obligation to divide up his estate right away, he grants the son's request (v.12). Since this was the younger of the two sons making the request, he would receive one third of the estate while his older brother would be entitled to eventually receive two-thirds.

Interpretation

Several powerful words and phrases are used in verses 13–15 to describe the way in which the young man destroys his life. He journeys into a distant country and squanders (scatter, strew, waste) his estate with loose living (riotous, foolish). After he spends everything, he is completely unprepared for the severe famine that occurs. As a result, he begins to be impoverished (destitute). His desperate circumstances result in his taking the only job he can find: feeding pigs. A Jew feeding pigs? A bad day and a bad life for sure! He is out of relationship with his father, and he needs to wake up.

Application

While Jesus sets up an extreme scenario, it is not uncommon to see a young person today decide to leave home to get out of his parents' house. Sometimes leaving home also results in leaving God. But the parable is about so much more than leaving. It is also about coming home. The crossroads question that Jesus has been leading His audience to throughout Luke 15 is, "What happens next when a person who has been out of relationship with God returns?"

Jesus also teaches about taking responsibility—a prerequisite to returning. In the video message, we used the analogy of having a flat tire to help us understand the urgency associated with taking responsibility. In other words, when one of the tires on my car is flat, fixing it always becomes a dominant priority. For the person who will be successful at taking responsibility, the lost son helps illustrate that three things must happen.

I must see change as being necessary.

On the day this lesson is being written, a professional athlete is very much in the news, because his life is crashing down around him. He appears to have an addiction problem, but he seems to be blind to it and in denial. He's been arrested. There have been accusations of domestic violence. He's been cut by the team that had been paying him piles of money. His parents can't seem to get through to him, and now his agent has cut ties with him. The young man probably hasn't hit rock bottom yet, but it can't be far away.

In our parable, it takes hitting rock bottom for the lost son to see his need to change. In verse 16, he gets so hungry that he becomes the Jew who wants to eat pig food! That's a rock bottom day for any self-respecting Jew! But then the verse also says, "and no one was giving anything to him." The owner of those pigs seems to be taking better care of his pigs than he is of his employee.

But then from the bottom of the pig pen, verse 17 says that the lost son "came to his senses." He finally awakens to the idea that his life didn't have to be the way that it had become. He realizes that his father's hired men have it much better than he does in that dirty pig pen. The people that work for his father always have plenty to eat. Our young man finally sees that a change is necessary.

I must take ownership of the problem—no matter whose fault it is.

The second key to taking responsibility is to take ownership of the problem. The lost son takes ownership in verses 17–18 of the text. He begins planning his return home, and he determines that he will use three powerful words when he meets his father. Verse 18 tells us that his confession will include the statement, "I have sinned..." We struggle with that one sometimes, don't we?

And did you notice the second part of this key step? It's the idea of taking ownership even when there may be the temptation to find someone else or something else to blame. The young man is in the pig pen, and he takes ownership of his bleak reality. Think about some of the places he could have attempted to place blame:

- His father—Why didn't my dad try to protect me from me? Why did he give me all of that money, especially if he knew I wasn't ready for it? Surely some of this must be his fault!

- The people who helped him waste his money—I had a lot of so-called friends when I was rolling in money. Surely they must take some blame for helping me waste it!

- The severe famine—That famine has to be partly to blame. Things never would have gotten this bad had there not been a famine!

- The people who still had money but wouldn't help him when he was down and out—If those folks had just given me a meal or two, it never would have been this bad!

- The guy who hired him to feed pigs—It sure seems like he could have taken a little bit better care of me than he did!

In taking responsibility, the lost son didn't try to play the blame game. The question for us is, do we blame or do we take responsibility?

I must determine to live obediently.

A plan never makes a positive difference until it is put into action. Verses 20–21 of the text reveal that the lost son came home and humbled himself before his father. He confessed his sin. He expressed that he was unworthy to be called a son. He determined to obediently return, no matter what that might look like when he got back home. How much less regret would we have if our priority could always be to live obediently?

The lost son made a purposeful decision to walk away. A loving God has blessed us with the freedom of choice, and sometimes we make unwise choices. What God wants, though, is obedient living.

Jesus paints a powerful picture of our God when He depicts God the Father as watching for and running to greet that returning son. He welcomes His son back, not as a hired hand, but as a son. And the celebration begins (verses 22–24)!

Conclusion

Is there a "flat tire" in your life today that has either stranded you spiritually or perhaps is preventing you from reaching your potential? If so, do you have the courage to take responsibility for it? If you do and if you will, you can know that God the Father is anxiously waiting to welcome you with open arms! God is always ready to be in a relationship with the person who will take responsibility.

Discussion

1. Explain why a Jew feeding pigs would be such a "rock bottom" event.

2. Who are some of the people that the lost son could have chosen to blame?

3. Why do we often have so much trouble saying out loud, "I have sinned"?

4. In the video message we talked about

some spiritual flat tires. Are there more specific names we could put on the spiritual "flat tires" that plague us most in the twenty-first century?

5. What do we learn about God from this parable, and how should that knowledge help us be more successful with taking responsibility?

Chapter 7

Serving

The Parable of the Sheep and Goats
{Matthew 25:31-46}
Justin Guin

One Main Thing

God has given each of us opportunities to serve Him. We must use these opportunities to minister to others, especially to fellow believers, as if we are serving Jesus Himself, for people in need represent Jesus.

Introduction

In Matthew's gospel, the evangelist records five discourses of Jesus (Matt 5–7; 10–11; 13; 18; 24–25). One theme woven through each discourse is the importance of genuine faith. In order to follow Christ, His disciples must demonstrate their faith with action. The religious leaders during Jesus' life were described by Him as "blind guides" (Matt 23:24) who cared more about their traditions than the principles on which their law was founded (22:38–39; 23:23). Such an attitude had serious eternal consequences because faithfulness demands serving God and our fellow man. How one responds to people in need has eternal consequences (25:46). Christ's disciples stand in contrast with the hypocrisy of the Jewish leaders in Jesus' time. Christians are people of service and compassion, not neglect and indifference.

In the twenty-first century, our world must see a compassionate, serving church. Paul reminded the Corinthians that the church is Christ's "ambassadors." As such, He makes His appeal through us (2 Cor 5:20). When we serve our fellow man, the church is a sounding board for the gospel to a world in need of salvation (1 Thess 1:8). Neglecting such opportunities signifies spurning the opportunity to participate in the mission of God. Such is the situation described in the Parable of the Sheep and Goats in Matthew 25:31–46.

Setting

The image of the sheep and goats is derived from common pastoral practice in Palestine. Sheep and goats grazed together during the day but at night the shepherd separated them. Sheep prefer the open air and goats need the warmth of a stable.

Also, sheep were worth more than goats and this may have influenced the portrayal of sheep as being righteous and goats as unrighteous. His audience would have been familiar with this pastoral process and its theological application (cf. Ezek 34:17).[1] Regarding the placement of right and left, it has been suggested this refers to the practice by the courts of placing the acquitted on the right and the convicted on the left.[2] The privilege of those on the "right hand" is attested in the Old Testament (Gen 48:13–18). In the Psalms, the "right hand" of God represents shelter from evil and a source of blessings for the faithful (Ps 16:11; 17:7; 18:35). In Matthew 25, those on the "right hand" of the Son of Man are given an inheritance of eternal life.

Interpretation

In Matthew, we are introduced to three parables which teach two principles: how to live wisely

---

[1] Craig Keener, *IVP Background Commentary: New Testament*, Olive Tree Bible Software n.p.; Leon Morris, *The Gospel According to Matthew*, PNTC (Grand Rapids: Eerdmans, 1992), 636.

[2] James M. Freeman and Harold J. Chadwick, *Manners and Customs of the Bible* (New Brunswick, NJ: Bridge-Logos Publishers, 1998), 470.

and the consequences of doing and not doing.[3]
Each stresses the responsibility of disciples and
the need to make preparation for the coming
judgment of the Son of Man. The final parable
brings this message to a climactic end with a
judgment scene. The Son of Man judges the
nations from His glorious throne. According to
Daniel 7:13–14, the Son of Man would reign over
the nations in an everlasting kingdom. In the Old
Testament, judgment of the nations was reserved
for the Lord (Isa 2:4; Mic 4:3).[4] In Ezekiel 34:17,
the Lord would be the one who separates the
sheep and the goats. Both the title "Son of Man"
and the task of judging the nations is assigned to
Jesus in this parable (cf. Matt 16:27; 19:28; 24:30).
While incarnated Jesus lived a lowly life but in this
passage Jesus is portrayed in His eternal glory
as He judges the nations. He comes in power to
inaugurate the final state of affairs.[5]

In this parable, the metaphor of the sheep and
goats is dropped in 25:34. The Son of Man directly
addresses the righteous, and notes their acts of

---

[3] Ben Witherington III, *Matthew* (Macon, GA: Smyth & Helwys, 2006), 458.

[4] Keener, *Background Commentary*, n.p.

[5] Morris, *Matthew*, 635.

service to fellow believers. Note the phrase "the least of these who are members of my family" (v. 40, NRSV). The list of deeds in the text follows standard deeds in Jewish ethics meeting the three basic human needs: food, shelter, and companionship. The righteous responded to those in need and did whatever the situation demanded.[6] Consequently, they inherited the "kingdom prepared for you from the foundation of the world" (v. 34, ESV). Inheriting something is a gift and not earned. Jesus is not advocating righteousness earned by works of merit.[7] Rather, righteousness is demonstrated by a lifestyle of ministering to others. This life is rewarded with an eternal relationship with the Son of Man.

In contrast with the righteous ones, those on the left neglected to meet the needs of others. They were guilty of sins of both omission and commission. Neglecting opportunities to serve others and respond to the Christian witness leads to damnation. Their inheritance was eternal punishment. God originally made no provision for eternal punishment. Once humans and fallen

---

[6] Craig L. Blomberg, *Matthew*, NAC 22 (Nashville: Broadman & Holman, 1992), 378.

[7] Morris, *Matthew*, 637.

angels chose to rebel then a place of punishment was prepared.[8] Contrast their eternal fate with that of the righteous ones. Those who are consigned to punishment have no one to blame but themselves.

Application

The church must be watchful for opportunities to serve, especially those who belong to the "household of faith" (cf. Gal 6:10). Souls in need represent Jesus. Thus, we must minister to those in need as if they are Jesus Himself. A genuine faith is a serving faith. This parable teaches several theological points that are repeated throughout the New Testament.

First, future judgment demands a life of service in the present. The judgment scene demonstrates that righteous deeds reap eternal rewards while neglect leads to damnation. While addressing the issues relating to the final resurrection in 1 Corinthians 15, Paul concludes with an exhortation to abound in the work of the Lord (15:58). Such a lifestyle is not lived in "vain" but will be fully rewarded.

---

[8] Blomberg, *Matthew*, 379.

Second, the church's righteousness is demonstrated through acts of service. When we neglect those in need or offer words instead of action, James asks, "What good is that?" (Jas 2:16). Such a choice is not the marker of a saving, genuine faith. In fact, James states such faith is "dead" (v. 17). In Matthew 25:31–46, this same form of neglect reaps eternal damnation. Only God can declare a person righteous through His grace. God's grace prepares us for service so that we can demonstrate this declaration of righteousness (Eph 2:10; 2 Tim 2:1).

Third, serving others is serving Jesus. Note how personal the church's ministry is to Christ. He uses the personal pronoun "I" or "me" twenty-three times in 25:35–43. Souls in need represent Jesus Himself. Therefore, we must take advantage of every opportunity to serve others. Such is following in the "footprints of Jesus" (Matt 9:36). The church is the hands and feet of Christ to serve a world in need.

Conclusion

The church must be servant-minded. God has given His people opportunities to do good for others. We must minister to people in need as if they are Jesus Himself. When each part of the body of Christ is doing their part it leads to the growth of the church (Eph 4:16). Such service pleases the Lord, and this is the aim of Christianity (2 Cor 5:9). The heart of Christianity is a relationship with the Lord, and this relationship is manifested in loving, sacrificial care for others.[9]

Discussion

1. How does the Parable of the Sheep and Goats relate to the overall context of Matthew 25? What is the emphasis of this parable?

2. What is the difference between those on the right hand and those on the left? How does serving our fellow man enable us to participate in God's mission?

3. In Matthew 25:40, Jesus refers to those who received aid as "brothers of Mine" (NASB). What responsibility does the church have toward fellow Christians? Do fellow believers have a greater priority than non-Christians? How does Galatians 6:10 help us understand this?

---

[9] Michael Green, *The Message of Matthew*, BST (Downers Grove: IVP, 2001), 263.

4. What does Jesus teach us about the eternal consequences of neglect? What are some ways we can take our Christian responsibility seriously?

5. How does God's grace prepare us for service? (cf. Eph 2:10)

Chapter 8

Kindness

The Parable of the Two Debtors
{Luke 7:41-42}
Travis Harmon

One Main Thing

If we will remember that we are sinners who have been saved by the grace of God it will cause us to treat other people with kindness and respect.

Introduction

The Parable of the Two Debtors is a short and often overlooked parable of Jesus.

"There was a certain creditor who had two debtors. One owed five hundred denarii, and the other fifty. And when they had nothing with which to repay, he freely forgave them both. Tell Me, therefore, which of them will love him more?" (Luke 7:41–42, NKJV)

Jesus loved to teach through object lessons, illustrations, and stories. We see it again and again in scripture that when Jesus needs to teach a lesson He uses something in His current situation as an illustration. Usually He does it to show people some hypocrisy that they are blind to and do not want to see.

In Luke 7, a Pharisee asked Jesus to eat with him in his home. The Pharisees were very religious. The word "pharisee" even means "one who is separated," indicating that they wanted to make themselves more holy than others. In the middle of the meal a sinful woman comes in and makes a spectacle of herself by weeping and wiping the feet of Jesus with her hair.

Setting

We have to remember they did not sit at a table the way we think of sitting at a table. Leonardo da Vinci's *The Last Supper* certainly does not represent the way a meal actually took place, and not just because in the painting they are all seated on the same side of the table. They would actually recline around the table and prop themselves on their left arm and eat with their right hand. (This is how John leans back on Jesus' chest to ask Him a question in John 14:25.)

As they all lay reclining around the table at this Pharisee's home, a woman comes in that is known as a sinner. In verse 37, the Bible says she was a sinner and everyone knew it, including the Pharisee. I do not know what her sin was. Each of us can make our guess but it was something that gave her a reputation as an undisputed and well known sinful person. This has to be utterly appalling to the Pharisee. He is an extremely religious person who is very concerned about his own reputation. He has invited Jesus to his own home for a meal and this woman comes in and makes a scene by washing Jesus' feet with her hair and tears. In my mind, Jesus and the Pharisee are most likely across from one another so they can talk. Because they are reclining (basically lying down) the woman is able to come in and wipe the feet of Jesus while He looks at his host, and the host watches this horrifying scene play out in front of him.

As the revolted Pharisee is watching this he thinks to himself, "If Jesus were a prophet, He would know that this woman is a sinner." It appears that he believes that if Jesus knew what this woman was He would be just as disgusted. He thinks Jesus should have rebuked her and sent her away because she is vile. But Jesus does not. In fact, Jesus calls the Pharisee by name and says, "Simon,

I have something to say to you." Simon says, "Say it"—something I bet he later regrets having said, since what Jesus has to say is not at all what Simon was expecting. Jesus tells the Parable of the Two Debtors and calls for Simon to be a judge over the two debtors. This is interesting because so much of what has just happened in the gospel of Luke is about judging. Look back over chapter 6 and especially notice verse 37. Here we find the famous section on "do not condemn" and the "beam in your own eye" passage. Then in 6:43 we have the "tree is known by its fruit" section that ends with "out of the abundance of the heart the mouth speaks." Jesus knew the judgmental heart of Simon before he even spoke it.

Jesus gives this parable as a way to set Simon up as a judge over the two people in the story. Simon judges that the the one that will love more will be the one that was forgiven the most. Jesus responds with, "You have rightly judged." I think in that statement Jesus is pointing out that in the parable Simon judges rightly, but in the situation between the "sinful" woman and himself he has not judged rightly at all.

Interpretation

I find it fascinating that in verse 44 Jesus turned to the woman. He looks at her but Jesus keeps talking to Simon and asks, "Do you see this woman?"

All this time Jesus has been looking at and talking to Simon while Simon has been watching this weeping woman wipe the feet of Jesus with her hair. Now Jesus turns away from Simon but continues to talk to him and asks, "Do you see this woman?" What a strange question! Yes! That is all that Simon has seen. There could have been an elephant beside Simon and he would not have seen it because he was watching every move this sinful woman made! He has watched her make a horrible scene at his house, at his meal, in front of Jesus!

"Do you see this woman?" In fact, the answer is, he did not see the woman. What Simon saw was a worthless sinner. What Simon saw was an interruption and a nuisance. He only saw a vile person that destroyed his special moment. He did not see a woman. He did not see a person. Jesus saw the person. Jesus saw the woman. Jesus saw someone of value, someone He was going to the cross to die for.

In 2 Peter 1:9, Peter mentions those who are "blind, forgetting that they have been cleansed from their past sins." I think this is what Jesus is telling Simon. Simon has forgotten that he also has to be forgiven. He forgot that in God's eyes, he is a sinner and no more or less valuable then the woman he was looking down on.

[Kindness]

Application

Imagine that one Sunday morning everyone in your congregation has invited several members of their friends and family to come to worship and for the first time they have all agreed. The building is packed and while the congregation is singing the first song you hear someone in the back openly crying. You turn your head and see a person who is known in the community as a drug dealer, prostitute, or the town drunk walking up the aisle. As they pass by your row you can smell the acrid aroma of last night's binge drinking still clinging to their dirty, disheveled clothing. The person passes by your row and, weeping, kneels at the communion table. How hard is it to imagine that some of the people in that scenario would be watching in horror?

What does real Christianity look like? It looks a lot like showing kindness and mercy to those that you think are beneath you. It looks a lot like seeing people and not just their problems. It looks a lot like remembering we are sinners who need to be saved by the grace of God, just like everyone else. It looks a lot like loving people more than we love our cultural or social norms and it looks a lot more like Jesus' response to sinners than Simon's.

Conclusion

I love how in verse 48, Jesus stops talking to Simon and talked to the woman for the first time. He says to her, "Your sins are forgiven." How amazing that must have sounded to her! I honestly cannot think of anything better than to have Jesus say to me, "You are forgiven." It is not the super religious Pharisee that gets that moment with Jesus, but the sinful woman.

Most of the time when we hear this story we imagine ourselves as the woman. In reality we may have been the woman at one time in our spiritual lives, weeping at Jesus' feet and begging forgiveness, but once we are forgiven, we forget that we were once vile sinners. As we mature, if we are not careful, we become the Pharisee. We become harsh and judgmental and look down on people we deem sinful.

"Amazing grace! How sweet the sound that saved a wretch like me! I once was lost, but now I am found; was blind, but now I see!" Jesus tells the woman to go in peace, but Simon has a lot to think about... and I believe we probably do too.

Discussion

1. Is the church for the saved or the sinners?

2. Does the church want real sinners? Or just, "people who would fit in well here"?

3. Who in our society (or church culture) do we not "see"?

4. Discuss the similarities between Simon the Pharisee and the older brother in the Parable of the Prodigal Son (Luke 15:11–32).

5. Read the Beatitudes in verses 20–26 of the preceding chapter of Luke. Can you read each verse and see either Simon or the woman contrasted? How much of chapter 6 do you see relating to this story?

6. What very interesting and important information is given to us in John 11:2?

Chapter 9

Living Ready
The Parable of the Ten Virgins
{Matthew 25:1-13}
Ted Burleson

One Main Thing

We must make preparations for the Lord's return. He could return when we least expect Him to do so. Are you ready?

Introduction

Evidently there are those, even in the church, who are unprepared for the Lord's return. Jesus told the Parable of the Ten Virgins to illustrate how some are prepared while others are not ready for Jesus to return. Many of us struggle with being unprepared for life. However, we must be prepared for eternity if we plan to spend it in heaven. Just as five of the young virgins were unprepared for the bridegroom, the hustle and bustle of life sometimes gets in our way of prioritizing spiritual things. The problem of taking care of the urgent while neglecting the importance of preparation is as real today as it was in the days of the ten virgins who were waiting for the bridegroom.

Setting

Weddings in the days of Jesus were very different from weddings today. First, the marriages were arranged. Sometimes, the bride and groom had not even met before the wedding. Second, unlike weddings today that last about twelve minutes, weddings in those days lasted a week. Third, invitations were sent out without a specific date for the wedding. A follow-up invitation would be sent when it was time to travel to the wedding. Note also, these were not just wedding guests, these virgins were the bridesmaids; they were in the wedding party. Please do not give the impression that resting was the problem; enough people already struggle with the guilt of not doing enough. Notice, all of the virgins "slumbered and slept" (Matt 5:25 KJV). This lesson is about being ready to meet the bridegroom, which for us is Jesus Christ at His second coming.

Interpretation

The ten virgins shared several things in common. They were all in the wedding party. They all went forth to meet the bridegroom. They all took lamps with oil in them. They all slumbered and slept. They all heard the midnight cry that it was time to meet the bridegroom.

In contrast, there was one significant difference among the ten virgins. Five of them demonstrated their wisdom by taking extra oil while five foolish virgins carried only their lamps and the oil contained in them with no reservoir of oil. In other words, five were prepared while five were unprepared.

Some readers express disappointment that the five wise virgins did not share. After all, we learned in kindergarten to share. Often Jesus' parables contain details that contribute to the story but are not intended to have a spiritual application. The overarching principle in this parable is readiness.

Others have complained that the Lord did not open the door for the virgins. His answer was that He did not know them. Of course, this illustrates the point that we must all be ready to appear before the judgment seat of the Lord. Since we do not know the day or the hour when the Lord shall come, we must be ready to meet the Lord at any moment in time.

Application

How do we stay ready for the return of the Lord? Real Christianity looks like the following scenarios. First, maintain a relationship with the Lord to assure that He will not have to say to us, "I do not know you." For example, Cameron is tempted to leave the commitment she made to the Lord when she was baptized into Christ. Her boyfriend is pressuring her to do things that she knows the Lord would not approve. Her close relationship with the Lord keeps her from giving in to temptation and remain dedicated to obeying Him. Stay close to the Lord and change the way you live on a daily basis.

Second, worshiping God on a regular basis helps us stay ready for the return of the Lord. Real Christianity can be illustrated by the example of Frank, a faithful Christian who loves to worship. Frank works ninety miles from his parents and his fiancée. When he gets off work on Saturday at noon, he can hardly wait to make that drive to see his loved ones. Never could Frank imagine saying, "You know, that's a long way and I'm really tired. Sunday is my only day off; I'll just stay here and not go see my family." Why? Frank loves his family and wants to spend time with them. If we love the Lord, we will want to stay near those who also love and want to worship Him. Worship is not just for Sundays; we study and pray on a daily basis, even today.

Third, real Christianity looks like being ready to be with the Lord at any moment. Jim was called to his lawyer's office for a routine meeting, at least he thought. As he walked into the office, a disgruntled former business partner shot Jim in the back five times, killing him instantly. How could Jim know that he was going to be killed? He didn't know, but he did live each day communing with the Lord in prayer and being ready to meet Him. Jim could have been foolish and unprepared if he was living a life of sin, but instead he was ready to meet the Lord. Although we are not his judge, there's little doubt that Jim is being comforted in Abraham's bosom, like Lazarus in the story of the rich man (Luke 16:22). If your life should end in death this night, will you be ready to meet the Lord?

Fourth, real Christianity looks like being willing to wait on someone you love. Have you ever been in a wedding? Let's say that the rehearsal and the dinner are on Friday night and that takes a total of about three hours. You are told by the photographer, "Be here at 10:00 a.m. for pictures." The wedding is not until 2:00 p.m. You have your picture taken countless times and eat a sandwich and notice that it is 12:15. You have almost two hours to wait, and you're dressed in your wedding garments. Why did you ever agree to be in this wedding? Because it is your best friend that is getting married and that friend asked you to be in the wedding. Likewise, because we do not know when the Lord is coming, some have been waiting on the Lord's return for decades. Just because He has not returned as of yet is not an indication that He is not coming (2 Pet 3:8–10). Waiting is difficult and Satan will use the delay to tempt you to be unprepared to meet the Lord. Do not give in to Satan, not for even an hour.

Finally, real Christianity comes with blessed assurance and confidence that we are ready to meet God. As a young preacher, I wept beside the bed of a godly, Christian woman who was so yellow with disease that she was in her last moments on earth. She gently said to me, "Son, do not cry for me. In a few minutes I'll be with the Lord and you will be left to deal with the problems of this world. I'm going to be with God." Sure enough, within fifteen minutes she was gone. She died with confidence and assurance because she had prepared for that moment for many, many years.

Conclusion

Are you ready to meet the Lord? Have you made the necessary preparation and are you maintaining your readiness? As a child, many of us went through fire drills, Civil Defense drills, and weather preparedness drills. We were practicing being ready. The alarm would sound when we were least expecting it, like a thief in the night (1 Thess 5:2). With racing heart and tired legs, we responded to the drill. However, what if it was not a drill? There is a time coming when each person on earth and those who have passed away (John 5:28-29) will hear the trumpet of God, the voice of the archangel, and be called to give an account of our lives. Are you ready?

Discussion

1. What was the real difference between the wise virgins and the foolish virgins?

2. Why do people often put off being prepared spiritually?

3. What is the connection between being prepared and going to heaven?

4. What is meant by the phrase, "I know you not"?

5. Recall James Henry Stanley's song, "Prepare to Meet Thy God." Note the words, "Careless soul, why will you linger, wand-ring from the fold of God? Hear you not the invitation? O, prepare to meet thy God." Why is this song often used as a song of encouragement/invitation song?

6. What are some concrete examples of being spiritually prepared to meet the Lord?

Chapter 10

Persistence

The Parable of the Persistent Widow
{Luke 18:1-8}
Matt Heupel

One Main Thing

As human beings we are a forced to live in a world that will treat us unfairly, but as Christians we cannot afford to give up.

Introduction

Jesus tells his parables within a specific context. Within that context lies the original meaning of the parable. The context for our parable begins in Luke 17:20 with the Pharisees asking Jesus about the coming of the kingdom. Jesus responds by saying that the kingdom can't be viewed as a onetime event, or something that they could take notice and say "there it is!" The kingdom of God was in reality right there in their midst (17:21). After revealing some things that must take place before and when the "Son of Man is revealed" (17:30), Jesus uses a parable to encourage his hearers to just keep on doing what they should be doing so that ultimately God will find faith.

Setting

This parable is applicable to us today because of the two characters involved. Within the city there was a judge. Under the Law of Moses each city was to have a judge who would make impartial decisions to make "righteous judgment" (Deut 16:18). These judges were warned to make sure that they did not pervert justice by accepting bribes or judging with partiality (Deut 16:19). These judges were to be careful because they were judging for God and not for man (2 Chron 19:6–7). However, the judge in this parable has obviously ignored such warning as he "neither feared God nor respected man" (Luke 18:2). Sadly, this may have been more of a true reflection of their current setting under Herod Antipas rather than a rare occurrence.

The second character of the parable is the widow. To be a widow in ancient times was just another way of saying that someone was hopeless. Without having a husband to defend her, a widow was typically the prey of those who were greedy and covetous. To protect these widows God had made laws to protect them against those who would seek to devour them, with warnings of punishments to be enforced (Exod 22:20; Deut 24:17; 27:19 and Mal 3:5). In Mark 12:39–41, Jesus even takes note of this mistreatment of widows. By understanding the main characters in the parable we will be more apt to understand and apply the parable to our lives in today's world.

Interpretation

We have noted that it wasn't uncommon for a widow in the ancient world to be abused; in fact it was probably the norm. So when Jesus uses this parable concerning a widow who had been mistreated and had gone before the judge, His audience understood full well the situation. As mentioned above, many judges of that day under Herod Antipas could not have cared less for God nor for what was right, fair, and just. Such was the case with the judge within this parable. Upon her first attempt to receive justice, the widow is refused. Time after time her request is denied; that is, until the judge grew weary of her request. He would have rather given in to her request than have to deal with her persistence. Jesus then shifts from the parable to its explanation. The judge was worldly and unrighteous, but God is righteous and just. If, therefore, we make our requests made known to God in prayer and are persistent with our petitions, He will certainly also give justice to those of us who are His.

The Pharisees had been looking and waiting for the coming of the kingdom of God. In their opinion, the kingdom would offer to them relief from the clutches of the Roman empire and restore the Jews to the glory days of David. They questioned Jesus about what would be the signs or evidence of the event. As they wait, what are they to do? Jesus answers that they should continue the practice of their faith in God and their petitions made to Him. When the Son of Man returns it will be sudden and without warning. Persistence in their prayerfulness and faith would ensure that they would be ready no matter when He might come. In this way when the Son of Man returns, He will find faith within His elect.

Application

"That's not fair!" How many times have we heard or uttered those words? The unfortunate fact is that while we live on this earth, life is not fair. Out of all of the promises of God there isn't one that reads "I promise to make your life on earth fair and just." Why is that? Is making our lives fair just something that is beyond God's reach? As Paul might say, "God forbid!" Life isn't fair because we live in a world that oozes selfishness and unrighteousness. We live within a world under the control of the devil (John 12:31). It doesn't matter where you live, when you live, or how well you live, the Christian will face injustice. Not only does the Bible promise these injustices, but it encourages us to be happy about them (James 1:2–4 and 1 Pet 1:6–7). So what can we do? How can we live in such a world that treats us so badly? We must follow the example of this persistent widow. She persisted in her request to the judge because of the treatment she was receiving from her adversary. I find it very interesting that Peter also describes the devil as our "adversary" (1 Pet 5:7–8). The widow's persistence was manifested in her "continually coming" to the judge. Likewise, our persistence in our faith can be manifested in our "continually coming" to the Judge, our Father in Heaven. In doing do, not only can we make known our requests to God on a consistent basis, but we are affected, as well.

First of all, persistence in prayer helps us remain focused. As long as I continually pray to God, I constantly remind myself of the power of God. The judge within the parable was unrighteous and was not God-fearing, yet he still had the power to control the situation. How much more power does our Heavenly Father have? It is really easy for us to lose our focus in this life because of all the ungodly, immoral people and unchristian situations with which we are placed. Yet if we are in constant communication with God, we can easily be reminded that our Judge spoke the world into existence, parted the waters, calmed the sea. The well-known preacher Adrian Rodgers once said, "God was with Noah, God was with Moses, God was with Elijah, God was with King David. We have it better than they did, GOD IS IN US!" If that isn't encouraging enough, notice the words of Paul to the Ephesians: "Now to him who is able to do far more abundantly than all that we ask or think, according to the power at work within us" (Eph 3:20). When we consider all our injustices, being persistent in our prayers will certainly remind us that God is able to deliver us!

Not only does persistence keep us focused on His power, it helps us to recognize that we are powerless. Why else would Jesus use a widow within the story? She is the most powerless of all people in the ancient world. No matter how hard she tried, she was powerless to resolve the situation herself and was at the mercy of her judge. How often do you feel helpless in this world? We are at the mercy of our circumstances. No matter how on top of things we are, we are never in complete control of things. It is only when we are persistent in our prayers that we recognize His awesome power in comparison to our own weakness. Yet with Him, even "when I am weak, then I am strong" (2 Cor 12:10).

Finally, being persistent with my prayers will help me remain focused on the task at hand. I may be powerless in the situation, but I can turn it over to God in prayer and allow Him to display His power. Until He acts, I can keep on doing what I know I need to do. I may not be able to control my circumstances, nor the attempts of my adversaries, and the hand I have been dealt may be unfair. I can still continue doing what I know I need to do. Jesus said that if I seek the kingdom of God first and His righteousness, then all of my physical needs will fall into place (Matt 6:33). This will enable me to focus on what is at hand and not on my injustices. Paul said, "one thing I do: forgetting what lies behind and straining forward to what lies ahead, I press on toward the goal for the prize of the upward call of God in Christ Jesus" (Phil 3:13–14).

Conclusion

At the end of the parable, Jesus reverts to the questions of the Pharisees concerning the coming of the Kingdom of God. If we remain focused on doing what we know to do, which is constantly making our requests made known to God, our religion morphs into a relationship. Having this type of relationship with our Father strengthens our faith, which in turn answers that question of the Pharisees. If we are doing what we know we are supposed to do and are focused on our faith, then it doesn't matter when He returns because we will be prepared. Hence the question that Jesus addresses to the Pharisees and those that hear His parable, "When the Son of Man comes, will He find faith...?" (Luke 18:8). If we are persistent, then the answer is yes!

Discussion

1. What kind of injustices face Christians today?

2. What are some ways in which we can remain persistent with our prayers, without using "vain repetitions/ empty words" that Jesus warns against (Matt 6:7)?

3. James 2:14–26 suggests that prayer alone is not sufficient. What are some things that a persistent prayer life might bring about?

Chapter 11

Hope

The Parable of the Lost Sheep
{Luke 15:1-7}
C. Wayne Kilpatrick

One Main Thing

Peter said it best: "The Lord...is not willing that any should perish, but that all should come to repentance" (2 Pet 3:9). The "all" means even the vilest outcast from society.

Introduction

Luke portrayed two sides of Jewish society in the setting of this parable and the two that follow. The "publicans and sinners" were rejected by the upper levels of Jewish society, while the "Pharisees and scribes" considered themselves holy, righteous, and better than the "publicans and sinners." These Jewish leaders quickly condemned others for trying to teach the publicans and sinners, but they themselves never evangelized the rejected. It seems that they were self-appointed critics following Jesus—standing afar just to find fault with His teachings and activities. On the other hand, those who had been treated as though they were some kind of contaminating disease were the ones who drew near to Jesus. They came to Jesus, not for His approval, but, rather, to learn more of God and His love for the lost. In so doing, many of them were converted. Matthew and Zacchaeus are good examples.

When we share the gospel with others, many times we encounter those who do their best to hinder our efforts. Sometimes it will be a family member or members of those being taught. Sometimes it may be a "good ole boy or girl" who does not want to lose a drinking buddy or a party mate. If Christ, the master teacher, was persecuted for this, who are we to think that the same thing will not happen to us sometime? Peter reminds us that "Christ suffered for us, leaving us an example, that ye should follow in his steps" (1 Pet 2:21). We will bear up under any hindrance in order to further the spread of the gospel, that the lost might be rescued; just as the sheep in our parable was lost, sought, found, and rescued.

Setting

The Parable of the Lost Sheep is one of three shorter parables within a larger parable. Each smaller parable is a self-contained unit that fits into the larger parable. Combined, they demonstrate the love that God has for the lost and His desire that they would come to repentance. "For God so loved the world, that He gave His only begotten Son, that whosoever believeth in Him should not perish, but have everlasting life" (John 3:16).

In this larger parable, there is the "lost sheep" which represents the "bewildered lost" that knows it is lost, but does not know how to get back to the flock. The second, smaller parable is of the "lost coin" and represents the "unconsciously lost" that is lost but does not know it. The first two shorter parables demonstrate there is something lost and it must be sought, found, and retrieved. The third parable represents those who are "willfully lost," one who chose to go astray, knowing the consequences, yet still going into sin. This "lost son" in the third parable still needed to be saved. It took his repentance and the Father's forgiveness to complete this third part of the larger parable.

With the three connected, they demonstrate the value of a lost soul. In the first, one out of one hundred sheep was lost and found. In the second, one coin out of ten was lost and found. In the third parable, one son out of two was lost and found. The parables combined show God's love and concern for their repentance. From the least to the greatest, all have need of salvation. From one of one hundred being lost to one of two being lost, the parables illustrate that salvation was for the least as well as the greatest. That which society counts as nothing God counts worthy of saving.

The parable of the "lost sheep" was fitting in the culture of the first century. Everyone in Palestine was familiar with shepherds and sheep. Perhaps this is why God mentions sheep in the Bible 188 times. The first family of mankind had a "keeper of sheep" (Gen 4:2). Abraham, Isaac, Jacob, Moses, and David were all keepers of sheep. Therefore, they were shepherds at some point in their lives. It is reasonable that Jesus would use things very familiar to His audiences as objects in His teaching.

Interpretation

In order to understand the meaning of Luke's Parable of the Lost Sheep, we must not confuse this parable with the lost sheep in Matthew 18 where Jesus used a similar illustration. These parables were told in different contexts and intended to make different points. Matthew shows Jesus as teaching against those who cause others to stumble. Luke shows Jesus as teaching on repentance. The parables pointed to two different meanings. We must understand parables according to context and purpose in order to get the correct meaning of the text.

Here, in Luke, the setting included publicans and sinners coming to hear the teachings of Jesus and Pharisees and scribes standing near and condemning what they saw. Jesus knew their thoughts and was prompted to give this parable along with the two that followed.

In verse 4, He asked a simple question: "What man of you, having a hundred sheep, if he loses one of them, does not leave the ninety-nine in the wilderness, and go after the one which is lost until he finds it?" So he searches and searches. He goes into the hedges, the byways, the wilderness, and the mountains looking for the lost, just as Christ was doing here. That was part of His ministry. "For the Son of man is come to save that which was lost" (Matt 18:11; Luke 19:10). He went to where the lost could be found, unlike the Pharisees and scribes who were not even the slightest evangelistically-minded. They feared contamination from any personal exchange with the publicans and sinners. The Pharisees and scribes thought themselves to be righteous because they had kept themselves "pure" from the lower classes of humanity. The Pharisee in Luke 18:11 said, "God, I thank thee, that I am not as other men are, extortionists, unjust, adulterers, or even as this publican," words indicating a self-righteous attitude. The Pharisees knew the law, but failed in keeping it: "All therefore whatsoever they bid you observe, that observe and do; but do ye not after their works: for they say and do not" (Matt 23:3).

Jesus, in a seemingly sarcastic move, allowed the Pharisees and scribes to think they were the saved of the ninety-nine sheep in the fold. He shames them by asking, if it were real sheep and one was lost, whether they would seek it until it was found. He then strikes a deeper cord in their hearts by illustrating that God the Father was seeking that which was lost. If God was looking, as any good shepherd would, why were they not caring enough to go and seek the lost?

In verses 5–7, He further points to the shepherd figure as being God or Christ or both. The shepherd is portrayed as taking the lost sheep, when found, and placing it upon his own shoulders and taking it to safety. This signifies the care that God has for the penitent sinner and how He pours His grace and mercy upon "that which was lost and is found." And when he arrives home with the rescued sheep he calls all of his friends to share in his joy over the returned sheep. God experiences the same joy over the returned sinner. Not only was God happy for the sinner now returned to the flock, clean and forgiven, but there was also rejoicing in heaven "over one sinner that repenteth" (Luke 15:10).

Conclusion

This parable magnifies the grace and kindness of God toward us sinners. He desires that we should be saved and that we should be willing to do as He did. This parable also demonstrates that we should be joyful when a sinner who was lost is returned to the fold. God teaches us His character so that we may be like Him. Let us seek, find, bring back, and be joyful.

Discussion

1. Why do people read this parable and draw so many different conclusions?

2. Is it possible that the different conclusions come because the reader does not know how to read a parable?

3. What is the real objective of Jesus in giving this parable?

4. How does this parable connect to the two parables that immediately follow?

5. What is the recurring theme in the three parables?

Chapter 12

Inclusion
The Parable of the Great Dinner[1]
{Luke 14:16-24}
Brad McKinnon

One Main Thing

There's something special, spiritual even, about welcoming outsiders—the marginalized and excluded. It's part of what it means to receive the Kingdom of God.

Introduction

Food and hospitality are prominent themes in the gospel of Luke. These motifs appear in the

---

[1] I have found the following books particularly helpful in my studies of Jesus' parables: Amy-Jill Levine, *Short Stories by Jesus: The Enigmatic Parables of a Controversial Rabbi* (New York: HarperOne, 2014); Alyce M. McKenzie, *The Parables for Today* (Louisville: Westminster John Knox, 2007); Eugene H. Peterson, *Tell It Slant: A Conversation on the Language of Jesus in His Stories and Prayers* (Grand Rapids: Eerdmans, 2008)

temptation narrative, the stories of Jesus' miracles, His sayings or teachings, and even His resurrection appearances (4:1–13; 9:12–17; 11:1–4; 14:34–35; 24:28–35, 41–43). In addition, Jesus was challenged for His social habits centering around the table. For example, He was accused of being a glutton and drunkard and criticized for eating with tax collectors and "sinners" (5:30; 7:34). And of course, many of Jesus' parables focused on food and hospitality. As one scholar has put it, you can find yourself figuratively eating your way through Luke's gospel.[2]

Setting

Jesus' parables in Luke are fascinating on many levels. For instance, most of them don't seem to be predetermined. Jesus is acting more like a village storyteller, than a preacher or teacher. Making His way from Galilee in the north to Judea in the south, Jesus travels from hamlet to hamlet and house to house telling stories. He crafts these stories or parables in response to questions, requests, accusations, and His own personal observations.

---

[2] Robert J. Karris, *Eating Your Way Through Luke's Gospel* (Collegeville, MN: Liturgical, 2006).

One such parable is the Parable of the Great Dinner in Luke 14. As the scene begins, Jesus is invited for Sabbath dinner at the house of a leader of the Pharisees. Folks are returning from worshiping together, but instead of celebrating what they had in common, everyone is watching Jesus suspiciously. Along the way, Jesus encounters a man suffering from dropsy or edema.[3] Even though it was the Sabbath, Jesus heals the man, establishing the principle that it's never wrong to do the right thing. As guests begin to file in for the meal, Jesus notices them scrambling for the most prominent seats. He warns, "Don't exalt yourself or you'll be humbled. But if you humble yourself you'll be exalted." Then, He turns His attention to the host and exhorts:

> When you give a luncheon or a dinner, do not invite your friends or your brothers or your relatives or rich neighbors, in case they may invite you in return, and you would be repaid. But when you give a banquet, invite the poor, the crippled, the lame, and the blind. And you will be

---

[3] Edema is a swelling of the organs and skin caused by the build up of fluid in the body's tissues. It can cause weight gain, severe pain, and difficulty with mobility.

blessed, because they cannot repay you,
for you will be repaid at the resurrection
of the righteous. (14:12–14, NRSV)

Ha! Jesus accepts the host's invitation and then proceeds to criticize the guest list! Obviously, Jesus was not above breaking social conventions now and again to make a point. In the process, however, He frames hospitality as a spiritual experience that brings a blessing in the life to come.

Here Jesus suggests four categories of those not to be invited and four categories of those to be invited. First, who shouldn't be invited? It's interesting that these are the people we're most likely to interact with socially—friends, siblings, relatives, neighbors. Why not invite them? Maybe because it's what's expected. Or, you might feel a familial responsibility. Too, there may exist an ulterior motive of some sort. But, what about those you're supposed to invite—the poor and those with physical disabilities? It wasn't unusual in the ancient world to think of the poor or disabled as cursed by God (John 9:1–3) and somehow religiously inferior (see Lev 21:18; 2 Sam 5:8). These sorts of folks certainly couldn't return the favor, and your association with them may harm your reputation in the process.

It must have made everyone in attendance uncomfortable to hear Jesus criticizing how the host filled the allotted guest spots. In those moments of awkward silence, sometimes we're tempted to speak out of turn. In our story, one of the invitees sitting with Jesus blurts out: "Blessed is he who shall eat bread in the kingdom of God!" "Indeed," you can almost hear Jesus saying, "let me tell you what the Kingdom of God is really like." Addressing His fellow guests, Jesus tells a story about a man hosting a great dinner.

Interpretation

In the parable, there are three groups of invitees to the dinner. First, there are the excuse makers who decline the invitation. One has just bought a field. One has bought ten oxen. Another has just been married. As many have recognized, these excuses mirror those in Deuteronomy 20, a passage that outlines the acceptable excuses for requesting leave from military service in Israel (v. 5-7). If you've built a house, go home and dedicate it. If you've planted a vineyard, go home and enjoy its fruit. If you're engaged to be married, go home and marry your fiancée. But how does the master of the house in our story respond to these sorts of excuses? Jesus says he reacted in anger. Apparently, even acceptable excuses for not helping to defend your community and country don't work in the Kingdom of God.[4] The second group are those who hang out on the streets and in the lanes—these match the four categories Jesus mentioned earlier (the poor, maimed, blind, and lame). These are the cursed. The worthless. The excluded. The untouchables. And the third group is made up of those found on the outskirts of town—at the highways and in the hedges. These are the outsiders and marginalized, who are not welcome in traditional political, social, and religious circles.

Application

So what picture does Jesus paint of the Kingdom of God in this parable? It seems there were some in Jesus' day who should have been ready for what was unfolding in His ministry. Unfortunately, they did not recognize it and respond favorably, apparently because it deviated from their preconceived expectations. Today, I wonder if those of us who have been privileged socially, educationally, and religiously would have fared any better in appreciating Jesus' purpose. On the

---

[4] John Donahue, *The Gospel in Parable* (Philadelphia: Fortress, 1988), 142.

other hand, how happy are those who have been excluded for so long to finally receive acceptance?

So what does real Christianity look like? It's an environment of inclusion—living life in community, where everyone has a place. This reminds me of the popular 1980s sitcom tagline, "Sometimes you wanna go, where everybody knows your name." There seems to be something deeply human about needing to feel welcome and included. However, much to our shame, the human family has also had a tendency to practice exclusion to the detriment of community.

So how do we practice inclusiveness? It may literally include creating worship spaces and services that are accessible to the physically disabled. It may include being intentional and taking active steps at being a guest-friendly church. It may include recognizing the imago Dei in everyone, despite the significance of social constructs like race and class. It may include recognizing the two greatest commandments: loving God and loving your neighbor. It may even include asking ourselves what it would really be like to take the teachings of Jesus seriously, especially those about some sort of reversal of fortunes: "Blessed are you who are poor, for yours is the kingdom of God. Blessed are you who are hungry now, for you will be filled. Blessed are you who weep now, for you will laugh" (Luke 6:20–21).

Conclusion

In the hours just before His death, Jesus acted as host rather than guest (Luke 22). One of the themes of the evening seemed to be inclusion. I think the personal pronouns are significant. "I have eagerly desired to eat this Passover with you." "Take this and divide it among yourselves." "This is my body, which is given for you." "This cup that is poured out for you ." The group seated with Jesus was in many ways a motley crew—some fishermen, a tax collector, an extreme nationalist, and a traitor to name a few—but they were all welcome at the table.

Likewise, disciples today gather at the table each week to better understand life in community. Despite our differences, we proclaim solidarity with Christ and with each other. Now, appreciating inclusion doesn't mean denying any expectations. After all, those invited had to respond favorably to participate in the blessings at the master's table. However, inclusion means just that—inclusion. Inclusion for the insider prepared to receive the invitation to the banquet, but also for the outsider who might not look the part or comprehend standard religious jargon. And yet still there is room, and the invitation still stands in order to fill God's house at the kingdom banquet. As I reflect on this parable, I'm reminded of the words of the marvelous poem by Jan Richardson:

And the table
will be wide.
And the welcome
will be wide.
And the arms
will open wide
to gather us in.
And our hearts
will open wide
to receive.
. . .

And we will become bread
for a hungering world.
And we will become drink
for those who thirst.
And the blessed
will become the blessing.
And everywhere
will be the feast.[5]

---

[5] Jan L. Richardson, "And the Table Will Be Wide" (excerpt), The Painted Prayerbook (blog), September 30, 2012, http://paintedprayerbook.com/2012/09/30/and-the-table-will-be-wide/. Used with permission.

Discussion

1. Why do you think Jesus suggests not inviting your friends, relatives, or rich neighbors to dinner? How would you explain the significance of such a reversal of typical social customs?

2. How would it change things in our homes, churches, and communities, if the ones typically excluded from our activities were the first ones to receive an invitation and the first ones we sought to serve?

3. What steps has your congregation taken to be a more guest-friendly church? What facilities and services are provided for those with special needs?

4. How well has the twenty-first century church done in taking Jesus' teachings on inclusion seriously? What improvements do you think can be made?

Chapter 13

Generosity
The Parable of the Rich Fool
{Luke 12:13-21}
Lucas Suddreth

One Main Thing

A spirit of generosity demonstrates that we are followers of Jesus and helps create opportunities for us to introduce others to our Savior.

Introduction

Hoarding gets a lot of attention these days. This behavior can manifest itself in people whether they are rich or poor, though the number of possessions many American households maintain may give the impression that hoarding is widespread in this prosperous society. We should remember that it is always sinful to value objects more than people.

Some Christians may exhibit a hoarding mentality in respect to their congregation. Sometimes, Christians can be church hoarders. Perhaps they will say, "This is my church, and you can come to my church as long as you don't get in my parking spot, and get in my way, and sit in my seat. This is mine and you can look but don't touch!"

Such behavior shows that we have forgotten our purpose as members of the body of Christ. Our mission is to introduce people to Jesus Christ (share) and help them follow Him (care). Being generous is a means to that end.

One way we can help the body of Christ grow is by exhibiting generosity. In doing so, we imitate our God, who loved the world so much that He gave His son (John 3:16). The Parable of the Rich Fool shows us the opposite of generosity.

Setting

Jesus was instructing the disciples on the need for faithfulness during times of persecution when a man abruptly interrupted Him with a demand for assistance: "Teacher, tell my brother to divide the inheritance with me" (Luke 12:13). The request this man makes, in actuality, is a directive. "Jesus, go do this!" Jesus responds, "Man, who made me a judge or arbitrator over you?" The reason why Jesus reacts so harshly is because this man was asking Jesus to quit teaching, to quit doing what He was sent here to do, and to settle a family dispute. During this time, it was shameful to take a brother to court because it was seen as "airing out the family's laundry."[1]

In verse 15, Jesus switches from addressing the man to addressing the crowd, instructing them to watch out for all types of covetousness. He says these things based on the man's actions. The motivation for this man's request was based in two things: greed and long-term security. Jesus is warning the people, "watch out, or you may find yourself more concerned about how unfair your life is than about your salvation."

Interpretation

Jesus then illustrates His point with a parable about a rich fool (v. 16–21). During a particularly prosperous time, this man decided to build larger storehouses without preparing himself for his ultimate fate. Upon first glance, some readers may think that the landowner had great business sense. The man had a bumper crop which he decided to save so that he could retire and sell

---

[1] Bruce J. Malina, *The New Testament World* (Louisville: WJK, 2001), 36–38, 43.

some of his harvest as needed. However, this is not Jesus' point at all. If we examine His audience, we know that during Jesus' ministry almost all of the believers were poor farmers and day laborers. They were not landowners!

The point Jesus is making is that the actions of this man were completely self-centered. As Fred Craddock describes this man, "He lives completely for himself, he talks to himself, he plans for himself, he congratulates himself."[2] The farmer sought to secure his future without any reference to God, which is why God labels him a "fool," signifying a person who rebels against God, or one whose practices deny God. He forgot that his life was on loan from God.

We may hope otherwise, but it is always God who has the last word. Jesus asks the landowner "the things you have prepared, whose will they be?" (v. 20). This rhetorical question should make us assess the value of accumulating possessions. This fool was what we might call a hoarder: his possessions defined his existence, taking on greater importance in his life than other people or even God.

---

[2] Fred B. Craddock, *Luke: Interpretation: A Bible Commentary for Teaching and Preaching* (Louisville: John Knox Press, 1990), 163.

Application

We should be sharers rather than hoarders. When it comes to the church, we want to grow to be the kind of people with a sharing mentality. We want to be generous with what we have so that others may be able to experience God's grace and love just like we do. We want to be like the church in Acts 2, where a spirit of generosity compelled believers to sacrifice their own possessions so that others could experience prosperity. They had this unselfish generosity that flowed from their realization that you can never out-give God. To become like the model church in Acts 2, we must, first of all, share within the church. From an early age we struggle with sharing. We all have a toddler mentality. We believe that everything we see is ours, and we see no reason to share our stuff! Yet the early church community realized that their things, their time, their food, and their money was not just theirs, but everyone else's too. They were sharers.

They were also in awe at what they saw and heard from Jesus and the disciples. The disciples were teaching and living out their belief of sharing everything they had and it shocked people. People couldn't believe they were giving away their things. Are we ever in awe at what we see and hear in the Bible? I pray we can always say yes. We need to share these moments of awe with each other. They had a generous heart towards other people and wanted to share this awe with others.

Sharing within our church is about sharing what we have with our church family. This is how we rejuvenate ourselves and others.

But, to follow the example of Jesus, we must share not only within the church but also through the church. In the book of Acts some people were wealthy, some poor, but they all had one thing in common: they were all rich in God. Therefore, they were able to live generously with whatever God had given them. They realized that God was everything they needed and so they gave happily. Some of the greatest acts of generosity that happen within the church take place without anyone knowing, such as anonymous contributions. We may never see the outcome of our generosity here on this earth, but we shall in the age to come. When we relinquish our bodies to return to the dust we enter into our forever home where we will be rewarded for those anonymous contributions.

Sharing through our church, and within the church requires that we share what we have with our community. We must be sharers.

Conclusion

We become real Christians when we believe that what we have is worth sharing; when we believe there is value in it; and when we believe in the power of what we have—the power of the Gospel.

Let us not forget that our mission is to introduce people to Jesus Christ (share), and help them follow Him (care). Being generous is a means to that end.

Discussion

1. Why do some people become hoarders?

2. How do you think a hoarding mentality affects people in the church?

3. What role does sharing play in the Christian life?

4. In what ways was the man in this parable foolish?

DEGREES DESIGNED
for
REAL WORLD MINISTRY

BACHELOR OF ARTS
The Bachelor of Arts is a 128-hour program designed with an emphasis on preaching and communication of the gospel. Includes Christian service mentoring and mission work each semester.

MASTER OF MINISTRY
The Master of Ministry is a 36-hour program that seeks to enhance the service and leadership of persons who are engaged in ministry.

MASTER OF ARTS
The Master of Arts is a 36-hour program that enables students to read and interpret biblical texts in their original languages. Students will engage in rigorous academic research.

MASTER OF DIVINITY
The Master of Divinity is a 75-hour comprehensive program that equips students for leadership in a congregation. Students will develop a holistic ministry plan that addresses the needs of a Christian community.

All programs are available anywhere in the world via Distance Learning

Office of Enrollment Services
www.hcu.edu 256.766.6610
PO Box HCU, Florence, Al 35630

OUR MISSION

Heritage Christian University

exists for the advancement of churches of Christ by

equipping servants through undergraduate and

graduate programs and continuing education. HCU

produces effective communicators, preachers, teachers

and missionaries for real-world ministry with a focus on

evangelism and a commitment to Scripture.

57564899R00074

Made in the USA
Charleston, SC
16 June 2016